Having a Ba Is a Beautiful Miracle of Love and Life

"Susan Polis Schutz remains one of the most popular poets in America, and her work touches virtually everyone."
Associated Press

"Susan Polis Schutz has taken us on a descriptive, revealing, magical journey from the pregnancy to the birth of her first son. I wholeheartedly recommend this book of poems to all who are either contemplating pregnancy or already embracing it. Through Susan's poetry, one can experience just what pregnancy feels like."
Kathy Smith
Noted authority on fitness and nutrition
Creator and star of bestselling
workout videos

"Susan Polis Schutz's popularity can be attributed to her ability to verbalize intimate, honest emotions shared but unsaid by most people. Her ability to write...of the deepest emotions and the most fragile and fleeting of moments strikes a responsive chord with readers. Stephen beautifully illustrates Susan's poems. They are a team and their books reflect this." **Woman's Day**

"Susan Polis Schutz and Stephen Schutz's book is one that every parent can enjoy and cherish as they reflect upon the doubts, fears, anticipation and lasting joy of birth. t s a treasure to be passed on to future generations to enjoy."
James E. Peron
Founder/Executive Director
Childbirth Education Foundation

Having a Baby Is a Beautiful Miracle of Love and Life

Designed and illustrated by
Stephen Schutz

America's best-loved poet
chronicles her thoughts and feelings
before, during and after pregnancy

Susan Polis Schutz

Blue Mountain Press ®
Boulder, Colorado

Library of Congress Cataloging-in-Publication Data

Schutz, Susan Polis.
    Having a baby is a beautiful miracle of love and life
    /Susan Polis Schutz ; designed and illustrated by
    Stephen Schutz.
        p.   cm.
    ISBN 0-88396-358-2   : $7.95
    1. Mother and child-Poetry.   2. Childbirth-Poetry.
    3. Infants-Poetry.   I. Title.
PS3569.C556H38 1992
    811'.54-dc20   92-10668
                                                       CIP

Library of Congress Catalog Card Number: 92-10668
ISBN: 0-88396-358-2

Manufactured in the United States of America
First Printing: September, 1992

This book is printed on fine quality, laid embossed, 80 lb.
paper. This paper has been specially produced to be acid free
(neutral pH) and contains no groundwood or unbleached pulp.
It conforms with all of the requirements of the American
National Standards Institute, Inc., so as to ensure that
this book will last and be enjoyed by future generations.

Blue Mountain Press ®

P.O. Box 4549, Boulder, Colorado 80306

CONTENTS

Dedicated to my three children,
Jared, Jordanna, and Jorian,
and to my husband, Stephen.

INTRODUCTION

The poems in HAVING A BABY IS A BEAUTIFUL MIRACLE OF LOVE AND LIFE truthfully reflect my feelings before, during and after my first pregnancy. This book was part of my diary; however, I changed so dramatically during the nine months that it seems as if parts of it were written by another person.

Before becoming pregnant, I was not very interested in having children or in children in general. I associated pregnancy with mysticism and fear; however, when I was pregnant, fear and misery dominated the nine months ~ very little mysticism. And after having our baby, I could not remember being miserable at all. Even my attitude on raising a child changed. While pregnant, I interviewed people to take care of our baby during the days when we would be working. My philosophy was that they could raise him as well as we could. However, when it came time to leave him with our new child-care person, we could not part with him. He desperately needed our love and presence, and we needed his. So for the first eight months of his life, our son accompanied us to work.

I found out that, despite how I felt before having a baby, I could combine being a mother with my career. In fact, with the new, overwhelming love for our baby, my personal life and my career took on a new and expanded dimension.

What a beautiful miracle!

Susan Polis Schutz

Today I woke up
feeling strange
but special
For the first time
in my life
I thought about the fact that I
could produce a baby
Out of me
from he
a little baby
Unbelievable

Sure all my friends
have had babies
but I never thought of myself
as a man's wife
or a child's mother
I am just me, leading
my own life
and in love with he

But today, I pictured
a child building sand castles
and it belonged to us

Why do I keep
putting off
having children?
Is it because
my career is
too time consuming?
Is it because
I don't want the
discomfort of
being pregnant for
nine months?
Is it because I fear
labor?
Is it because I
cannot picture myself
as a
mother?

When will I be ready
to have a child?
Was I ever ready for high school?
Was I ever ready for college?
Was I ever ready for my career?
Was I ever ready for anything
that happened to me?

Should
I have a child
now?
It would probably be so cute,
and it could
live in the
empty room
near ours.
But should I
have a child
now?
It will
mean months of
nausea
and interference
with my
career and
life.
It will
mean
some pain,
and then a lifetime
of sharing another
person with us.
Am I ready
for a child?

Many
women I know
have told me that
they never felt
complete
until they had
their first
baby
I don't understand
this
Why can't women
feel complete
in themselves
like men
do?

I see so many women
whose lives
revolve entirely around their children
Everything they do
everything they have
everything they want
everything they dream
is for their children
This is not good
for the women
nor is it good
for their children
Both women and their children
need to develop
their own selves
with their own interests
with their own goals
with their own lives
I hope that when the time comes
I will be able
to find a proper balance
where I can be a great mother
and an individual woman
whose identity is not lost

I have never been
able to do two
important things
at once
I am working
hard at my
writing career now
It would be impossible
for me to concentrate
on raising a child, too

had a
discussion
with a group
of women
They wanted to know
why I wanted
to have children
when the world
is so overpopulated
Since I could not
come up with
a great answer
they thought I
should not have
a baby
I thought
about this
It would be
great to see
what kind of
person would
come from
the two of us
but that
seemed too
egotistical...

It would be fun
to watch
and help our child
grow from a baby
into an adult
No, this was not
the reason either
And then
all of a
sudden
I realized that
bringing forth
a new life
would be an
absolute miracle
I realized that
in this unstable world
love is so important
and the best reason of all
to have a baby is that
a baby would be
someone else to love

The test is positive.
It's what?
It's what?
It's what?
Me?
No, it must be wrong.
It must be wrong.
My name is
Susan Polis Schutz.
I'm a writer.
I'm not grown-up enough
to have a baby.

First month
of pregnancy

How will a
child fit in
with us?
We keep late
hours and
eat sporadically
We are selfish
catering only
to each other's
whims
We live with
and for each other
How will a third
person fit in?

Second month
of pregnancy

Why
do I keep crying?
I'm not really depressed
Probably it's just that
I'm so very tired
In fact I'm sort of happy
especially when looking at you
but I can't seem to
stop crying

Second month
of pregnancy

Why
did I take that
damn allergy pill?
Had I known
I was pregnant
I would rather
have continued
to sneeze than
to take a chemical
which might hurt
my child
The allergy doctor told
me to take two pills
every day, and that most
medicines are safe during pregnancy
What does he
care?
It's not his baby

Second month
of pregnancy

I was planning
on buying
some of the beautiful
new winter clothes
I've seen
but now
I can't
and I guess
I kind of
resent that

Third month
of pregnancy

I can still hide from myself
the fact that
I am pregnant
because I am not that fat
As soon as I
outgrow my jeans and sweaters
I will realize that I
am pregnant
and then I will
really be scared

Third month
of pregnancy

Last time I waited
two hours to see the doctor.
Today I thought I was smart.
I called the nurse right before
my appointment to see if he was
on schedule.
The nurse said, "Yes, you're next."
I rushed to the doctor's office
and checked in...
and waited
and waited
and waited.
I went to the desk and
told them that I was supposed
to have been next.
They said that they were sorry,
and that there were five people
in front of me.
"Your doctor is very popular
and everyone waits for him,
and they feel that he is
worth it.
He's a very important man,
you know."
"I'M AS IMPORTANT AS THE DOCTOR,
AND I WON'T WAIT FOR HIM."

Third month
of pregnancy

Round face
pale complexion
no waist
indigestion
Exhausted
nauseous
moody
weak
That's the new
pregnant
me

Fourth month
of pregnancy

I can no
longer zip up
my jeans
but I refuse
to give them
up
so I
wear my
jeans
unzipped
and held together
by a diaper pin
But now I
need a very
long top
to cover
the mess

Fourth month
of pregnancy

Our baby
will be
very loved
by parents
who will guide it
teach it
and cuddle it
But it will not
be the only
important part
of our lives

Fourth month
of pregnancy

Our baby
will be a
child of
the mountains
It will be
able to run
free among
the spruce trees
close to the sky
It will be loved
by its family and friends
the plants and animals
Our baby
will be
a very happy
child
of the mountains

Fourth month
of pregnancy

It is now
four months
I feel so
healthy
Sometimes
I get scared
because I
have absolutely
no symptoms
of pregnancy

Everyone keeps
asking me if I
feel the baby
moving
I don't really
know
And then I get
worried
because they
say by this
time I am
supposed to
feel
life

Fourth month
of pregnancy

I am very
protective
of my big
stomach
Someone bumped
into me and
I screamed
It really hurt
I know the baby
is well covered
Still it is vulnerable
and I will try hard
to keep protecting it

Fourth month
of pregnancy

It must not be
fashionable to be
pregnant nowadays.
In one week,
though I saw many children,
I did not see one
pregnant woman.
Where are all
the pregnant women?
Are they forced
into feeling self-conscious
because of society's
attitude towards them?
Being pregnant
is not a sickness.
It is the highest
form of being.
It is time
to honor pregnant women
rather than to
force them into
seclusion.

Fifth month
of pregnancy

We went to
New York City for a vacation~
museums, plays,
concerts, restaurants,
shopping, galleries,
bookstores~
but I did not
have the energy
to complete a day's
activities.
I needed to nap
every three hours.
Though I tried,
it was almost
impossible to
forget that
I was pregnant.

Fifth month
of pregnancy

Will our baby
have sky-blue eyes
that examine
and understand
and that melt
with sensitivity
like his
father's do?
Will our baby
get lost in
his own genius
concentrating on and
deciphering
new subjects
like his
father does?...

Will our baby
appreciate the
solitude and beauty
of the outdoors
like his
father does?
Will our baby
face and conquer
every challenge
becoming stronger and
wiser with each one
like his
father does?
Will our baby
be as
truthful and
good and
honest and
gentle and
unselfish and
loving and
beautiful
as his
father is?

Fifth month
of pregnancy

Now I know that
I have been
feeling a new life
It started
out
feeling
like little
tiny flutterings
that were almost unnoticeable
Now the movement
is much more intense
It actually
feels like
there is someone
poking me from the
inside
out

Sixth month
of pregnancy

Today
I jumped
from the
hard kick
I received
in my stomach
I wonder if an
active "kicker"
proves to
be an
active
person
If so
I like the
kicking

Sixth month
of pregnancy

Whenever
anyone sees me now
they treat me as a pregnant woman
no longer a career woman
no longer sexy or attractive
just another pregnant wife
Whenever anyone speaks to me now
they speak to me as if I were their mother
They no longer talk to me about
world affairs, business, careers, or goals
but strictly about diapers and babies
and family life
Why can't people treat me
as the person I have always been?

Seventh month
of pregnancy

Today my doctor
placed a stethoscope
on my stomach
and told me to listen
to the baby's heartbeat
I heard a slight drum beat
The doctor and the nurses
were so excited
but I could not equate this sound
with the heartbeat of the baby
who is inside of me
I tried hard to picture the baby
with this heartbeat and
for a few minutes I actually
believed this miraculous event
But by the time I got home
I thought it was all a dream

Seventh month
of pregnancy

I am afraid to
feel excitement
about having a baby
because if there were
something wrong
it would be such
a traumatic disappointment
This way, I will try to
repress the excitement I feel
about my pregnancy
and then hope to be
very pleasantly
surprised

We are not
going to buy
anything
for the
baby
or plan
anything
for the
baby
until we
meet
it

Seventh month
of pregnancy

People think
I have a
cold attitude
towards my
unborn baby
because I
don't love
being pregnant
and because
I speak of a child-care person
to care for the
baby when it
is born...

I love my
child as all
other mothers-
and fathers-to-be love theirs
but I feel
very defensive
when people
think it is cruel
for a new mother
to have a career
of her own
They assume
that all good mothers
must sit at
home twenty-four hours a day
taking care of
their babies
I feel
cold towards
these people
who criticize
me
and I cannot explain
to them
that I love
my baby as
much as they
love theirs
and that my
baby will be
at least
as wonderful
as theirs

Seventh month
of pregnancy

Natural childbirth~
the idea is nice
and so are the classes
Imagine
seeing the birth
of your child
But truthfully
I would just rather
wake up
and find out
I had a baby

Eighth month
of pregnancy

No, I'm afraid
I'm not the
earth mother
that it is so
popular to be
I am not so
excited about
the pain of
labor and delivery
I am not convinced that
my baby will not be as
healthy as the
next baby because
I will be using baby bottles
in addition to nursing
I will use
throw-away diapers
and anything
else to
make things
easier
No, I'm afraid
I'm not the
earth mother
that it is so
popular to be

Eighth month
of pregnancy

I think
I have a
smart baby
inside of me
It kicks
punctually
the minute
I lie down
When I'm very
active, the baby is
quiet
When you put your
hand on my stomach
to feel the kicking
it always
stops
Already it knows
how to get
our
attention

Eighth month
of pregnancy

I absolutely detest
being pregnant
I am no longer an
independent woman
free to run
about the world
If I honestly could
believe that there is a
real baby inside me
I probably would not feel
so badly about
giving up all the
physical things
I love to do

Ninth month
of pregnancy

Knowledge Versus Emotions

I have read so many books
I know that after six weeks
the fetus is the size of a walnut shell
and the important organs are forming
I know that after eight weeks
the fetus has a face, arms, hands and fingers
legs, feet and toes
I know that after twelve weeks
the basic structure of the fetus is finished
I know that at twenty weeks
the fetus is approximately
one foot long
I know that at twenty-four weeks
the fetus opens and closes its eyes
I know a lot of details about
the daily development of the fetus
and what it looks like
but somehow this knowledge
has not gotten through to my emotions
My knowledge tells me that there is a
well-formed human being
growing inside of me
almost ready to be born
but my emotions do not
understand or believe this

Ninth month
of pregnancy

I am getting
bigger and
bigger
My legs
hurt so much
that often
I cannot
walk
I am very
tired and
need an
enormous
amount of
sleep
But as
soon as
the baby
kicks
I forget about
everything
and cannot
wait
to see
it

Ninth month
of pregnancy

You and I do everything
together
We never separate
Always we are together
Will our baby
join us?
Will there
be three of us
together
at all times?

Ninth month
of pregnancy

I feel so strange
because I do not know when
I'm going to have the baby
Each day I wake up
saying, "Is this the day?
I hope not, because I'm too tired,"
or "I have all these appointments.
Today would not be so good,"
or "It is so beautiful and I feel great.
Today would be perfect."
But no, I'm still pregnant
I guess I have no say about
when the baby will be born
When it is ready, it will
let me know
regardless of
whether or not I am ready
It would be nice to have it
soon, though, so I can
return to a normal life

Ninth month
of pregnancy

I am a prisoner
of my own body
My stomach is so huge
I cannot even put on my shoes
My thighs hurt so
I cannot walk
My legs cramp
I cannot stand still
The baby kicks my ribs
I cannot sit in a chair
I am so tired
I cannot finish most activities
I am so big and puffy
I hate to look at myself
My body is king
I am its helpless servant

Ninth month
of pregnancy

Lying in the
mountain sun
tired and uncomfortable
waiting
I stared at the
ground beneath me
A little two-leaf clover
peeked out under the
tall blades of buffalo grass
It looked so tiny and fragile
so helpless
The little two-leaf clover
and our little baby soon to be born
I love them both

Four days after
due date

Oh my God
I think I'm in labor
Twenty minutes apart
Fifteen minutes apart
Ten minutes apart
It is not as bad as
I thought
except that I know
it will get worse
and I cannot back
out now
No one can bail me out
Oh my God
I am really scared
This is it
No one can help me
share the pain
Oh my God
I am really scared

One week after
due date

"Yes, I'm in labor now."
"Susan Polis Schutz."
"Boulder, Colorado."
"May 23."
"No."
"No."
"Yes."
"Yes."
"How many more questions?"
"No."
"Of course."
"I had measles, mumps, mononucleosis."
"Penicillin, dust, cats."
"Can you please take me to my room? I'm
very uncomfortable."
"Yes, I'll pay when I leave."
"Yes, I'll sign for that."
"Yes, I have insurance,
but what if I didn't?
Would you make me have
my baby in the street?
Never mind.
This is absolutely ridiculous. I demand that
I be taken to my room now. I'll answer these
stupid questions later."
"No, I want a private room. I requested it
this morning."
"No, I won't wait a half hour down here. Are
you crazy?"
"I'll tell you what, instead of sitting here
talking to you, you may visit me after I have
my baby. I'm getting the hell out of your
stupid office."

                    The morning of
                    the birth   53

A most
amazing
incredible
phenomenal
thing~
After being
in very mild labor
for twelve hours
I went to my doctor
He examined me
and told me to go
home quickly to
pack my bags
I was to have
a cesarean section
Totally unprepared
for this, I
could only cry
because I
was scared
Two hours
later, I
checked into
the hospital...

My family
waved to me
as I was
wheeled to the
operating room
The cesarean section
took thirty minutes
and my
baby was
finally
here
A most
amazing
incredible
phenomenal
miracle

One hour after
giving birth

WAKE UP

It's a boy
You had a boy
Wake up, Susan
do you hear me?
You had a boy
Susan, you had a boy
Hello, Susan
Did you hear me?
You had a baby boy

One hour after
giving birth

o you
want to see
your baby boy now?
Do you want to see him?
No, not now thank you
I'm too weak
Do you want to see
your baby boy now?
Do you want to see him?
A little later, please
I'm too weak
A little boy?
Who is he?
Did he really come from me?
Is he okay?
What does he look like?
Is he healthy?
Yes, hurry, please
let me see my
little boy

One hour after
giving birth

Jared Polis Schutz
a whole little person
a miracle
from God
to Stephen, to me
to the world

Jared Polis Schutz
a beautiful little person
eight healthy pounds
delicate light skin
soft red cheeks
huge bubbly ocean-blue eyes

Jared Polis Schutz
a precious little person
who will share
our days
and nights
our life
our love

One day after
giving birth

Baby
don't cry
Please
don't
cry
We love
you
Baby
please
please
please
don't
cry
We love
you

One day after
giving birth

I am
so afraid to hold him
He is so fragile
How do I nurse him?
How do I know when
he is full?
How do I burp him?
How do I stop his crying?
How do I diaper him?
All of a sudden I am a mother
but no one showed me
how to be one
I am so afraid I will
do something wrong
Please teach me how to
care for my baby

> One day after
> giving birth

I am
so tired
and weak
I have no patience
for anything
Everything annoys me ~
the baby's crying
the door slamming
the stain on the rug
the scratch on the record
the pain in my stomach
everything ~ anything ~
Will I ever be
my real self again?
I'm so very
weak

One week after
giving birth

"POSTPARTUM BLUES"

"Postpartum blues"
Surely there is such a thing
but what a misnomer
It is exhaustion
It is physical weakness
How dare people reduce
this result of a very
traumatic experience
to just the "blues"

One week after
giving birth

Little son
you look at
me so in need
of reassurance
I smile with
love
and you smile
back happy and
secure
I feel like I always
have to look at you
so that I don't
miss one of your
glances
leaving you all
alone in this new
world

Three weeks after
giving birth

He looks at us
and smiles
He knows
how much
we love him
We smile
back at him
and his eyes
light up
and radiate
He is
only a tiny baby
but he is a
sensitive human
being
experiencing his
first love

Three weeks after
giving birth

Your father gives you
the same sincere attention
that he gives me
Your father treats you as a person, not a baby
just as he treats me as a person, not a female
Your father responds to your cries and needs
just as he responds to mine
Your father puts your demands before his
just as he does with mine
Your father is totally honest with you
just as he is with me
Your father loves you completely
just as he does me
And we both love your father dearly
for he is everything
that is beautiful
to both
of us

Four weeks after
giving birth

I thought
I loved my husband
with all
the love
I could possibly have
but now
a whole new love
   (which I never knew existed)
towards our baby
has been born
I am overwhelmed
by the emotional
warmth
beauty
and love
I share with
my husband and our
little child

    **Four weeks after
    giving birth**

Asleep
in my arms
startled by a noise
he raised his little head
and looked at me
He grinned with love
as his eyelids closed
and he fell back to sleep
I grinned with love
as my eyelids closed
with
tears

Five weeks after
giving birth

We sit here
among the wildflowers
completely peaceful
overwhelmingly thankful
in total disbelief
It is really over!
I am no longer pregnant
The operation is over
No more huge stomach
or bloated face
I will be able to walk fast again
I will be able to play again
It is really over!
I am no longer pregnant
We have a beautiful healthy baby
sleeping right next to us
He too is completely peaceful
among the wildflowers
Life is truly
a miracle

Six weeks after
giving birth

Everyone: "Susan, I am so sorry
    that you had to have a
    cesarean section."
Me: "Why are you sorry?"
Everyone: "Well, you didn't get the
    chance to see your baby being born."
Me: "So what?"
Everyone: "Well, it's just so beautiful and
    meaningful."
Me: "To me, the beautiful and
    meaningful part is that a new life
    has been born, and he is from us
    and will be loved by us forever."
Everyone: "Sure, that's true, but it would
    have meant that much more if you
    saw his actual birth."
Me: "Do you love your mother,
    father, brother and husband?"
Everyone: "Yes."
Me: "Well, I'm so sorry."
Everyone: "Why are you sorry?"
Me: "Because you didn't see
    their actual births."

**Two months after
giving birth**

I love
him so much
I want to
protect him from all
possible frustrations
He screams
because he cannot turn over
He cries
because he cannot crawl
He yells
because he cannot find his thumb
He falls
because he cannot sit up
I try to help him
do all these things
because
I love him so
but he does not
like my help
He needs to do things
all by himself
like the first time
he lifted his own head
and afterwards, grinned
at us for five minutes
I love
him so
and for this reason
I should not protect him from all
possible frustrations

Three months after
giving birth

He cannot talk
yet we understand each other so well
I know when he wants to eat
I know when he wants to sleep
I know when he is happy
I know when he is not
When he looks at me
with his piercing eyes
I know exactly how he feels
I look at him with love
and his eyes glisten
He looks at me with love
and my eyes tear
He cannot talk
but we understand each other so well

Three months after
giving birth

I never dreamed
how much I
could love
my little son
When we rest
in the grass
his thin arms
hold on to me
so tightly
His round floppy cheeks
rest softly
on my chest
and his tiny
red lips
lie open in
a most angelic way
I look at him
and I cannot stop
kissing him
I never dreamed
how much I
could love
my little son

Three months after
giving birth

AGE

People ask me
"What is the best age
to become a new mother?"
I think that the best age
to become a new mother would be
after you have had
many experiences in life
after you have shed
the hedonistic, egotistical
stages of your life
and when you are ready to go
beyond yourself and
reach out to other people
with a sincere love, respect, caring
and understanding of their needs

POSTSCRIPT

After having our first child, and much to my surprise, I loved being a mother. Though there was an added responsibility to our lives, we could not imagine life without this wonderful new love.

We worked many hours for the next few years and were fortunate to be able to take our baby with us. He traveled with us, hiked with us and was with us all the time.

We decided to have more children. My feelings during my second and third pregnancies were the same as during my first pregnancy, except that I knew what to expect physically and mentally. I knew that with a lot of work I could be a good mother, so I didn't have apprehensive feelings about becoming one. However, after seeing how overwhelming my love was for my son, I wondered whether I had any more love left for another child. But after I had my second child, a daughter, and again after I had my third child, another son, I immediately found out that I had plenty of love left for them. I was amazed at how much love is stored inside of us just waiting to blossom.

Now, as I look at my three beautiful children and think about my past pregnancies, it is hard for me to relate to my negative feelings about the physical aspects of being pregnant. And since my children are so different from one another, raising each of them continues to be a new and fascinating experience. As my first son, about whom this book was written, prepares to enter college, I can reflect on the pleasures of raising him, and I am so proud of the incredible human being that he has grown up to be.

I wish that all parents would slow down and spend time with and enjoy their children, because they grow from twenty-one inches to six feet tall in a very short time. Without putting in a lot of work, effort, time and love in raising children, mothers and fathers will miss out on the deepest joys of being parents.

Yes, it is often difficult, tiresome and hard to be a mother, and there is never a rest from being a mother. But helping my children grow up to become competent, caring, sensitive, successful, happy individuals is the most important thing I could ever do. It is, by far, the most loving and rewarding.

ABOUT THE AUTHOR AND ARTIST

Susan Polis Schutz began her writing career at the age of seven, producing a neighborhood newspaper for her friends in the small country town of Peekskill, New York, where she was raised. Upon entering her teen years, she began writing poetry as a means of understanding her feelings. For Susan, writing down what she was thinking and feeling brought clarity and understanding to her life, and today she heartily recommends this to everyone. She continued her writing as she attended and graduated from Rider College, where she majored in English and biology. She then entered a graduate program in physiology, while at the same time teaching elementary school in Harlem and contributing freelance articles to newspapers and magazines. Today, Susan is perhaps the world's best-selling poet. She is known for her honest and sensitive poems which strike a universal chord with both men and women around the world.

Stephen Schutz, a native New Yorker, spent his early years studying drawing and lettering as a student at the High School of Music and Art in New York City. He went on to attend M.I.T., where he received his undergraduate degree in physics. During this time, he continued to pursue his great interest in art by taking classes at the Boston Museum of Fine Arts. He then entered Princeton University, where he earned his doctoral degree in theoretical physics. Today, Stephen is famous for his mystical airbrush and watercolor blends, his beautiful oil paintings and his innovative, unique sense of design.

It was in 1965, at a social event at Princeton, that Susan and Stephen met, and their love affair began. Together, they participated in peace movements and anti-war demonstrations to voice their strong feelings against war and destruction of any kind. They motorcycled around the farmlands of New Jersey and spent many hours outdoors with each other, enjoying their deep love and appreciation of nature. They daydreamed of how life should be.

Susan and Stephen were married in 1969 and moved to Colorado to begin life together in the mountains, where Susan did freelance writing at home and Stephen researched solar energy in a laboratory. On the weekends, they began experimenting with printing Susan's poems, surrounded by Stephen's art, on posters that they silk-screened in their basement. Their love of life and for one another, which they so warmly communicate, touched the public. People wanted more of Susan's deep thoughts on life, love, family, friendship and nature presented with the distinctive, sensitive drawings by Stephen.

In 1972, Susan and Stephen's first book, COME INTO THE MOUNTAINS, DEAR FRIEND, was published, and history was made in the process.

When Susan was pregnant with their first child, she wrote about her feelings before, during and after her pregnancy. This journal was published as a book in 1976. Due to a demand from women who wanted to know the truth about being pregnant, Susan and Stephen revised and expanded the poems and art in this book into a new edition entitled, HAVING A BABY IS A BEAUTIFUL MIRACLE OF LOVE AND LIFE.

This book is Susan and Stephen's eleventh book of poetry. It follows their most recent bestsellers, LOVE, LOVE, LOVE; TO MY DAUGHTER WITH LOVE, ON THE IMPORTANT THINGS IN LIFE; and TO MY SON, WITH LOVE.

In addition to their books, Susan and Stephen's poems and illustrations have been published on over 200 million greeting cards and have appeared in numerous national and international magazines and high school and college textbooks.

Susan and Stephen live in Colorado with their children. They spend all of their time together. They live in an atmosphere of joy, love and spontaneous creativity as they continue to produce the words, the poems, the rhythm and the art that have reached around the world in many different languages and cultures, opening the hearts and enriching the lives of more than 500 million people. Truly, our world is a happier place because of this perfectly matched and beautifully blended couple, Susan Polis Schutz and Stephen Schutz.